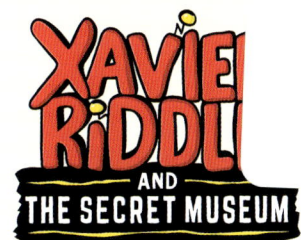

I am Theodore Roosevelt

adapted by Brooke Vitale

PENGUIN YOUNG READERS LICENSES
An Imprint of Penguin Random House LLC, New York

Penguin supports copyright. Copyright fuels creativity, encourages diverse voices, promotes free speech, and creates a vibrant culture. Thank you for buying an authorized edition of this book and for complying with copyright laws by not reproducing, scanning, or distributing any part of it in any form without permission. You are supporting writers and allowing Penguin to continue to publish books for every reader.

© and TM 9 Story Media Group Inc. All rights reserved.

Published in 2020 by Penguin Young Readers Licenses, an imprint of Penguin Random House LLC, New York. Manufactured in China.

Visit us online at www.penguinrandomhouse.com.

ISBN 9780593096369   10 9 8 7 6 5 4 3 2 1

"Woo-hoo! Swings, here I come," Xavier shouted, racing toward the museum playground.

"It's fort time, Dr. Zoom!" Yadina called, clutching her stuffed turtle.

Xavier and Yadina's best friend, Brad, followed close behind. "I want the—" Brad stopped short. "Spider!" he shouted, pointing at the monkey bars. "Ah! No-Go Zone!"

Brad raced away from the playground.

"No-Go Zone?" Xavier asked, following his friend.

Brad nodded. "I do *not* like creepy-crawly things. When I see one, I mark the spot on my map as a No-Go Zone so I know not to go there again."

Xavier looked at Brad's map. There was a big *X* over the museum doors, with a picture of a worm.

Next to the fountain was a picture of a frog. That was crossed out, too.

"Now a hairy, scary spider," Brad said, putting another big *X* on his map. "The playground is *definitely* a No-Go Zone."

"Uh, Brad," Yadina said. "Everywhere is crossed out."

"Yeah, there's nowhere left to play," Xavier added.

Brad shrugged. "Well, if the museum got rid of all the trees and flowers, there wouldn't be anywhere for the icky bugs to hide."

Xavier shook his head. "I'm not sure that's a good idea." If they couldn't go where the *X*s were, where *could* they go? Suddenly, he had an idea. "To the Secret Museum!" he shouted.

The friends raced to the Secret Museum. Inside, they found a hat sitting on a podium.

"A hat?" Brad asked, studying it. "Do you think it scares away spiders?"

Before Xavier could answer, a hologram appeared in the room. "Look!" Xavier cried. "Theodore Roosevelt! That's who we're going to meet!"

"Do you think he can help me find somewhere safe to play?" Brad asked.

"Only one way to find out," Xavier answered. The friends placed their hands on Berby. With a great burst of light, they were sent back to New York City in 1865.

As they arrived, a little mouse ran into the room.

"No-Go Zone!" Brad shouted, racing for the exit.

Before he could get far, a young boy charged through the door. He was wearing a hat just like the one they had seen in the museum. "Has anyone seen a mouse?" he asked.

Yadina nodded and pointed to the corner of the room.

Bending down, the boy scooped up the mouse. "Thanks!" he said, turning to the friends. "I'm Theodore. But you can call me Teddy."

Teddy lifted his hat in greeting. As he did, a frog jumped out from under it.

Brad backed away—right into a water jug. He reached to steady the jug and saw a snake inside. "No-Go Zone! No-Go Zone!"

"You've got some funny pets, Teddy," Yadina said.

"Oh, they're not pets," Teddy said. "These are wild animals. They belong outside. They're part of nature, and they need space to live and grow. I was on my way to find them a new home. Want to come?"

A few minutes later, the friends found themselves on a city street.

"What's going on over there?" Xavier asked, pointing at a park.

"That's where the mouse, frog, and snake used to live," Teddy said. "Now they're putting up a building."

Brad looked at the animals Teddy was holding. He might not like creepy-crawlies, but it *was* sad that they had lost their homes.

Xavier looked around. "Maybe this tree could be their new home?" he asked, pointing to a small tree growing on the sidewalk.

"Or what about that garden?" Yadina said, seeing a small patch of grass in front of a house.

Teddy shook his head. "Too small. They need lots of space, with grass and shade and fresh water."

Just then, a carriage rattled down the street. Its wheels clacked noisily against the road. Brad looked down at the animals. "Hey, the snake looks kind of . . . scared," he said.

"Just like you were with that spider, Brad!" Yadina said.

Brad nodded. The spider had been scary, but it couldn't really hurt him—not the way the carriage could hurt the snake.

Brad was still thinking about the scared animals when he heard Teddy say, "I think this might be the place!"

Looking up, Brad saw that they were standing in a giant park.

"Whoa! This park is amazing!" Xavier cried.

Teddy nodded. "Isn't it great? Let's look for a place for my animal friends to live."

Brad, Yadina, and Xavier followed Teddy down a tree-lined trail.

"These trees are awesome," Xavier said.

"And a perfect place for the mouse to live," Teddy said. "Plenty of shade, seeds, and good dirt for its den."

Kneeling, Teddy gently set down the mouse. The creature took one look around and scurried off into the grass.

Suddenly, Brad heard Yadina shout, "Over here!" Yadina was standing beside a big pond. "Dr. Zoom and I think this would make the perfect *pad* for the frog," she said, grinning.

Teddy smiled as he lifted his hat. The frog hopped into the water.

"Glad you're happy with your new home, little froggy," Brad said.

The friends continued to make their way through the park. Soon, they found themselves in a quiet, rocky area.

"It's so calm here," Brad said. "Hey! Maybe this would be a good place for the snake?"

Teddy nodded. "The snake will love living here where it's quiet."

He leaned down and tipped over the jug the snake was resting in. He gave the jug a little shake, but the snake refused to move. "Hmmm. I think it's still scared."

Taking a deep breath, Brad kneeled down and looked in the jug. "I know this is scary," he said. "I'm not too sure about all this nature stuff, either. But I think you'll like it here if you just give it a try."

Brad waited. Finally, the snake slithered out of the jug and onto the rocks.

"You did it, Brad!" Yadina cheered.

Brad smiled, proud of himself. Then his smile faded. "What if this park gets torn down, too? Like their last home?"

"It won't," Teddy said. "This park is protected. That means people can visit, but they can't build here."

Hearing that made Brad feel better. "Are there more parks like this?" he asked.

Just then, Berby appeared.

"Guess we're about to find out!" Xavier said.

Brad, Yadina, and Xavier grabbed hold of Berby. There was a bright flash, and a basket appeared under their feet. The friends were in a hot-air balloon 41 years later . . . with Theodore Roosevelt!

Teddy had grown up to be president of the United States. And he had turned all the land below them into national parks!

"I created those parks to protect special places," he said. "No one can build anything there, so the plants and animals are safe."

"Whoa!" Yadina said, pointing at two bear cubs playing in the grass below them. "Look at that!"

As Brad watched, a bald eagle soared past the balloon and landed on its nest.

"I get it," Brad said. "Plants and animals need space. But that spider on the playground didn't have its own space. It's not safe."

Brad looked at his friends. It was time to go home.

The friends reached out and put their hands on Berby. A moment later, they appeared on the playground.

"C'mon," Brad said. "We have to find that spider."

"But isn't this a No-Go Zone?" Xavier asked.

Brad blushed. "Yes, but the spider is so much smaller than me. It needs its own space way more than I do."

As Brad made his way to the monkey bars, a kid knocked into the spider's web. The spider fell to the ground.

Brad raced over to help. Leaning down, he put the spider safely in the jar and walked it over toward the trees.

"So, where should we play?" Xavier asked when the spider was safe.

Brad grinned. "Anywhere we want! I'm going to change the No-Go Zones to Whoa-Go Zones! Places where we need to be careful because there are plants and animals. They need space to live and grow, just like Theodore Roosevelt taught us!"

And with that, the friends raced off to enjoy the playground.